Introduction

James is one of the few books of the Bible focusing the practical outworking of our Christian faith. In today's culture it would undoubtedly have been presented as an 'in-depth dynamic seminar on Christian Living', led by none other than the Bishop of Jerusalem, brother of Jesus, and probably subheaded: 'How to deal with... trials, temptations, riches, lust, sin, prejudice, self-sufficiency, poverty; and how to develop... patience, wisdom, prayer, good works, a controlled tongue and much more!' This is a practical how-to book on Christian living. Forthright and pulling no punches, it confronts, challenges and calls us to be committed to not only hearing the Word, but being doers of the Word also.

Its emphasis is vital Christianity, characterised by good deeds, an upright character and a faith that works. The necessity for faith is not minimised, but James insists that real faith produces positive results, undergirded by core values demonstrated in ethical behaviour. His goal is to bridge the gap between belief and behaviour, claims and conduct. He recognises in all of us the tendency to hear God's Word but the failure to put it into practice. In common vernacular James is saying, 'Don't just talk the talk, its time to walk the walk.'

Today we are inundated with so much hype, spin and high gloss. The products we buy and the services we use come with extravagant claims, guaranteeing to change our mundane lives for the better. We are promised whiter than white clothes, instant nutritional meals, faster cars, improved health, financial freedom, no more bad hair days, and much more. How often we are disappointed, as those who promise so much deliver so little. James says it is time for us to stop making the 'Christian' claims and time to deliver the 'Christian' goods the world is waiting to receive. Professing to believe in God, claiming to have all the right answers, then contradicting it with our lives, is nothing short of humbug and hypocrisy.

Of the three James' mentioned in the Bible, rather than James the son of Alpheaus, or James the son of Zebedee, brother to John, it is widely accepted by competent scholars that the writer of this epistle was most significantly James the brother of Jesus.

Accepting that fact, here was a brother who had been with Jesus from His earliest years, and had observed Him at the closest quarters from childhood to adulthood in all the cut and thrust of sibling rivalry, family life and growing up together.

As a blood relative of Christ, he was an eyewitness of the daily interaction and everyday routine activities. Who better than James, from his intimate experience of the background of Jesus' life as well as His public ministry, to reveal to us the important keys for daily Christian living? What he had witnessed in his brother Jesus and had now come to experience through faith for himself was the demonstration, application and practice of the Christ-life Jesus had outlined in His Sermon on the Mount.

We are not sure when James came to recognise his brother Jesus as the Son of God, but during early years he carried doubts about His divinity. John records, 'For even his own brothers did not believe in him' (John 7:5). They were unwilling to acknowledge one amongst them as the long-awaited Messiah, not an unexpected reaction among vying siblings, but the impact of His faultless character and peerless life was not lost on them. Now many years later, having been deeply and indelibly impressed, James encapsulates in this short epistle the essence of the Christ-life in practice.

COVER TO COVER BIBLE **STUDY**

7 SESSIONS FOR SMALL GROUP AND PERSONAL USE

James
FAITH IN ACTION

CWR

Trevor J. Partridge

Copyright © Trevor J. Partridge 2004

Published 2004 by CWR, Waverley Abbey House, Waverley Lane, Farnham, Surrey GU9 8EP, UK. Registered Charity No. 294387. Registered Limited Company No. 1990308. Reprinted 2008, 2009, 2010, 2012, 2013, 2014, 2017, 2018.

The right of Trevor J. Partridge to be identified as the author of this work has been asserted by him in accordance with the Copyright, Designs and Patents Act 1988 Sections 77 and 78.

All rights reserved. No part of this publication may be reproduced, stored in a retrieval system, or transmitted, in any form or by any means, electronic, mechanical, photocopying, recording or otherwise, without the prior permission in writing of CWR.

For list of National Distributors, visit cwr.org.uk/distributors

Unless otherwise indicated, all Scripture references are from the Holy Bible: New International Version (NIV), copyright © 1973, 1978, 1984 by the International Bible Society. AV: The Authorised Version.

Concept development, editing, design and production by CWR.

Front cover image: Roger Walker.

Printed in the UK by Linney

ISBN: 978-1-85345-293-2

Contents

5   Introduction

9   Week One
Life stresses and strains
James 1:1-18

15   Week Two
Saints under pressure
James 1:19-27

21   Week Three
Are you prejudiced?
James 2:1-13

27   Week Four
Faith on the move
James 2:14-25

33   Week Five
The taming of the tongue
James 3

39   Week Six
To thine own self be true
James 4

45   Week Seven
Patience is a virtue
James 5

51   Leader's Notes

Introduction

We know James did come to faith and that he became a pillar in the Early Church. Paul names him first among the three pillars of the church in Jerusalem (Gal. 2:9) and from a very early stage he occupied a leading position in the church there, becoming its first bishop (Acts 12:17; 21:18; Gal. 1:19). He is described as the leader and chief spokesman for the apostolic council in Acts 15.

James is a key book, not only because of its content but also because of its author. It is probably the earliest letter to the young Church, and written by one of the Church's first pastors, concerned and burdened with the everyday issues the scattered flocks confronted. He is writing to the twelve tribes dispersed among the nations and his anxiety is not so much about their theology, but the implementation and demonstration of a living gospel. It was not to people who had arrived in their Christian walk, but to those still on a steep learning curve that he wrote, those struggling to match their newfound belief with their everyday behaviour.

This epistle is not theological theory or repetition of what had been heard or taught, but the deep impact of the outworking of the Christ James had witnessed and experienced.

This is a book full of wisdom, deep, living, lasting wisdom, and James encourages us to be full of this wisdom, then to follow its dictates.

Are you ready for the first session of the James seminar? Let me suggest that you read the whole book at one sitting, four times if possible – there are only five short chapters. If possible, read it once in the NIV, once in The Living Bible, once in the J.B. Phillips translation and finally in *The Message*

WEEK ONE

Life stresses and strains

Opening Icebreaker

Identify four pressures that are part of your daily lives. Get into twos to compare notes and to share why they are pressures.

Bible Readings

- James 1:1–18
- Matthew 4:1–11
- 2 Corinthians 11:22–29; 12:7–10
- Philippians 4:11–13

Opening our Eyes

In his opening chapter, James highlights pressure points in daily living that lead to stress and strain if left unresolved. I describe them as 'stressors' – pressures that bring stress. He then gives underlying principles in facing them realistically. I call these 'stress and strain busters'. Let's consider the first four stresses and strains.

1. Trials and Adversity (1:1–4, 12) are the challenges life throws at us. In difficult times, our attitude and response make all the difference. Our natural reaction is to grumble, complain and resent them, however we have a divine resource to draw on to sustain us through them, a joy drawn deeply from the wells of salvation (Isa. 12:3). James says 'Consider it pure joy', that is, accept with happiness everything that comes your way. J.B. Phillips puts it like this: 'Don't resent them as intruders, welcome them as friends! Realise that they come to test your faith and to produce in you the quality of endurance.' Usually we count it joy when we escape adversities, but patience is developed and character tested and forged in the fiery furnace of adversity. Don't rejoice in the trial itself, but in God who is not overtaken by it, who specialises in turning tragedy into triumph and setbacks into springboards.

Stress and strain busters: Patience and Perseverance (vv3–4)

2. Decisions and Choices (vv5–8) are part of everyday life, from early morning until our head hits the pillow at night. Even then, we lie awake wondering if we've done the right thing, but it's often too late to reverse the decision. We have all made wrong decisions. James says circumvent that worrying and obviate the negative consequences. How? By stopping before we make those decisions to take a few moments banishing doubt and asking for God's wisdom that

Life stresses and strains

WEEK | ONE

is freely available to all His children in all circumstances. Don't ask God to bless your choices after you have made them, get the facts, don't be in two minds, seek God's discernment then take time to listen for His response.

Stress and strain busters: Wisdom and Discernment (v5)

3. Status and Wealth (vv9–11) are shrines at which many worship today. One of the first questions usually asked is, 'What do you do and where do you live?' Society places great importance on position and possessions. James gives perspective as to where true wealth and significance lie, humility of heart. It's our position and riches in Christ that count, not how we are viewed in contemporaries' eyes. Whether rich, poor, lowly or elevated, humility of heart is of highest significance in God's eyes. What you wear or drive doesn't represent your status before God. We are not to be partial to the wealthy nor prejudiced to the poor.

Stress and strain busters: Humility and Meekness (vv9–10)

4. Temptation and Sin (vv13–18) are inescapable in our fallen world. The pressure and influence of evil is all around, yet James says that resisting and overcoming temptation is a matter of character and choice. Make no mistake – no one is above temptation, but be sure of this, we are all capable of resisting it in Christ's strength (4:7). Sin's origin is in the desires of the human heart. Temptation itself is not sin, it becomes sin when we allow ourselves to be enticed into embracing it by indulging our own desires. The old children's chorus put it, 'Yield not to temptation' If you have, as someone has said, 'admit it and quit it'. Now!

Stress and strain busters: Vigilance and Alertness (v16)

Discussion Starters

1. Share some of the pressures you are currently facing that you discussed in pairs.

2. Look at the passages 2 Corinthians 11:22–29, 12:7–10 alongside James 1:1–4 and discuss the relationship of grace and joy, strength in weakness. Can you relate your own life experiences to these?

3. Think of some other biblical examples as well as Paul of those who were patient in adversity.

4. Define wisdom and discuss whether it is right to ask God for wisdom (not yet revealed) if we have not consulted and taken on board what is contained in the oracle of wisdom, His revealed Word

Life stresses and strains

WEEK ONE

5. Why is it that so much significance is given to status and wealth and acquisition? Read the Philippians 4:11–13 passage and discuss contentment.

6. What do you think are some of the characteristics of humility? (See Philippians 2:5–9.)

7. Explore the idea of temptation not being sin. In the light of James 1:13 are we tempted by the devil or by our own carnal desires?

8. Think through and identify some of the enticements we face.

Personal Application

Developing skills in Christian living is an ongoing process. We will either cave in under the pressures of life and end up defeated and stressed with less than God's best, or respond to the resources God has provided that James outlines. *The Message* puts it like this: 'You know that under pressure, your faith-life is forced into the open and shows its true colors' (James 1:3). Always remember that adversity is the door to opportunity. The opportunity to develop patience, receive wisdom, show humility and remain vigilant. Learn to embrace these qualities and allow their true colours to shine through.

Seeing Jesus in the Scriptures

The teaching of James closely follows that of Jesus' Sermon on the Mount where He taught the be-attitudes or as Billy Graham once put it, 'the beautiful attitudes'. They are in fact the correct attitudes to life that bring with them the blessing of God. Jesus not only taught them, He exemplified them by His life. James having witnessed them first hand, heard them expounded by the master teacher and experienced them for himself, outlines and underlines them for us.

WEEK | TWO

WEEK TWO
Saints under pressure

Opening Icebreaker

Have a mirror available and get volunteers to look into it and then turn away, asking them to describe how they look. Then read James 1:23–24. The volunteers should now look at someone else's face and turn away, this time describing how that person looks.

Bible Readings

- James 1:19–27
- Psalm 32:6
- Matthew 23:1–7, 23–28
- Luke 12:16–20
- Ephesians 4:25–27
- Galatians 6:1–5

Opening our Eyes

Last week we started looking at pressure points, 'stressors', in James 1, and we continue this week with the chapter to complete the remaining three James highlights, with their 'stress and strain busters'.

5. Anger and Temper (vv19–21) when unresolved, erupt like a volcano in an outburst of sharp words and hostile feelings. Not only that, they rob us of God's righteousness into the bargain. That doesn't mean to say we won't feel angry, but James says anger should not control our actions or determine our words. We should learn to control our anger and measure our response. There is no room for temper tantrums and sharp words in the Christian life. Learn to bite your lip, listen a lot, say little, show self-control, so other people won't have this kind of influence over your life. Let God's Word take a hold of your heart to calm you down. Jesus said, 'For out of the overflow of the heart, the mouth speaks' (Matt. 12:34). Remember, confrontations pass, but words leave scars for a lifetime.

Stress and strain busters: Self-control and Christ-control (v19)

6. Compromise and Self-Deception (vv22–25) are often the paths of least resistance – the easier option in the face of difficult choices. There is a price to pay of unpopularity and rejection when we go against the tide and speak up against injustice. Sometimes the risk seems too great. James says do what you know is right, don't see what's wrong, turn a blind eye and walk away. Don't get caught up in other people's deceptions by knowing about them and choosing to ignore them. When we do what is the right thing according to God's Word, by looking each day into His daily mirror, and not compromising what it reveals, guess what, we get blessed!

Look regularly into the mirror of God's Word and let it reflect what's really going on in your life. The story is told of a woman who suspected her husband of cheating on her. One day she saw him put something into a barrel of sawdust. After he had left the house she ran to the barrel, and in a heightened state of anxiety, pulled out the hidden object, blew off the sawdust and not realising she was looking into a mirror exclaimed, 'So that's the old witch he's going with.' Remember this, a mirror only reveals what is in front of it.

Stress and strain busters: Honesty and Integrity (v22)

7. Self-interest and Personal Ambition (vv26–27) are the hallmarks of modern culture. Conversations are riddled with self-centredness and self-focused bragging. Anyone who claims to be Christian and can't control his self-embellishing tongue is self-deluded. If you talk a good game, but do little to achieve a result, your claims are hollow. A recurring theme of James is self-interest and personal ambition. Who does it remind you of? The Pharisees, and Jesus didn't have much good to say about them did He? It's no good proclaiming the virtues of your beliefs, without down-to-earth involvement with the needy and powerless. How involved are you with the bereaved and fatherless? Put legs to your words, get your religion on the move, lay personal ambition and indifference to one side, stop talking and start doing.

Stress and strain busters: Kindness and Goodness (v27)

In the next few weeks' study, we want to move on to explore the 'stress and strain' busters for handling and overcoming these pressures of daily life.

Discussion Starters

1. Share some of the things that make you angry and describe how you deal with your anger.

2. What are some harsh, sharp or loaded words that are often said in the heat of the moment?

3. How do you feel about the idea of just listening and saying nothing? Is this self-control or repression?

4. Identify some of the things that we can often turn a blind eye to in our work environment.

Saints under pressure

WEEK TWO

5. Think of some Bible characters who stood up for their convictions and wouldn't compromise. Share your own experiences.

6. Look at Luke 16:12–20 and explore the predominant personal pronoun in this parable and God's conclusion.

7. Explore together the subject of ambition. Can ambition ever be good or other than self-centred, and if so when?

8. Is there a project your group could get involved in to do something practical for the widows and fatherless in your church or community?

Personal Application

Prayer is at the beginning and ending of this book. James' practical advice and down-to-earth insights are sandwiched in prayer. Tradition tells us that on the death of James they discovered that his knees were worn hard as a camel's through his constant habit of prayer. Some commentators say that even in life he carried the nick-name 'old camel knees'. Pray together about learning to handle well the seven pressures outlined in James 1.

Seeing Jesus in the Scriptures

Jesus never had to withdraw, or apologise for, any statement He made. He knew how and when to use words, choice words. He not only preached and proclaimed them, He also painted wonderful word pictures in parables peppered with colourful illustrations and rich insights. He held the crowds spellbound and enthralled as He portrayed an intriguing tapestry of the new kingdom with dramatic effect and vivid imagery. On other occasions He affirmed good men and witheringly exposed the hypocrites, the bigoted and outwardly religious. He was found in quiet conversation with individuals or His disciples, encouraging, comforting, supporting, chastising, confronting and dispensing words of life and wisdom. No wonder He could say, 'The words I have spoken to you are spirit and they are life' (John 6:63). The writer of the Proverbs poetically put it like this, 'A word aptly spoken is like apples of gold in settings of silver' (Prov. 23:11).

WEEK | THREE

WEEK THREE
Are you prejudiced?

Opening Icebreaker

Discuss how you feel about the current debate on asylum seekers, economic migrants and illegal immigrants.

Bible Readings

- James 2:1–13; 4:1–6,10
- Ecclesiastes 2:24–26
- Matthew 19:16–30
- Luke 10:30–37
- 1 Corinthians 1:26–31

Stressors: Status and Wealth

Stress and strain busters: Humility and Meekness

Opening our Eyes

Having highlighted the pressure points, James now expands on the keys in learning to handle them in everyday life, the 'stress and strain busters'. As we allow these qualities to develop in us, they will take the 'stress and strain' out of living. Rather than striving not to succumb to the strong pressures that are put on us daily, we will begin to flow in the power and poise these qualities bring.

James picks up immediately on the issue of *status and wealth* that brings with it favouritism, prejudice and finding favour with others. Echoing the words of his brother Jesus, 'Blessed are the poor in spirit' (Matt. 5:3), James asks the rhetorical question, 'Has not God chosen those who are poor in the eyes of the world to be rich in faith and to inherit the kingdom he promised to those who love him?'(2:5). How easily we are impressed with status, wealth, fame and the trappings of success. How susceptible we are to outward show and appearance, so often preferring to identify with successful people rather than apparent failures and losers. The celebrity culture pervades our society. We elevate the privileged and despise those beneath us on the social and economic scale. After all, who wants to be seen as a failure or to be consorting with losers and outcasts?

This, James says, is partiality and has no part in active faith. The apostle Paul put it like this in our reading in 1 Corinthians, 'But God chose the foolish things of the world to shame the wise; God chose the weak things of the world to shame the strong. He chose the lowly things of this world and the despised things – and the things that are not – to nullify the things that are' (1 Cor. 1:27). It would seem that, if anything, Jesus focused on the rejects, the poor, the powerless and the dispossessed.

Are you prejudiced?

He did not court celebrity and notoriety, but was to be found with 'publicans and sinners'.

So don't discriminate, James says, between rich and poor, the 'haves' and the 'have nots'. Take God's perspective, reject partiality and show humility by loving and serving rich and poor equally. How? He zeros in again on the words of Jesus – by practising *the royal law*: 'Love your neighbour as yourself', treat others as you would want to be treated yourself. That's the right way to neutralise the superiority of status and wealth and to dissolve partiality and prejudice. Love knows no boundaries of discrimination or barriers of prejudice, but enables us to graciously accept people as they are in a spirit of humility and meekness, whether influential or disenfranchised, whether lowly or elevated.

He comes back to this again in his fourth chapter, underlining the key truth, in verse 6, 'God opposes the proud but gives grace to the humble' so, he goes on, 'Humble yourselves before the Lord, and he will lift you up' (v10). James is more concerned with humility of heart, and the inner characteristic of meekness of spirit, than he is with outward show and appearance.

His final thought on the matter, in verse 12, is don't judge, but be willing to show mercy through impartiality, acceptance and grace. How? Deal a death blow to pride, be magnanimous to all, accepting all, loving all and serving all in *meekness of spirit and humility of heart*, out of your gratefulness in having experienced for yourself mercy when you deserved judgment, and life when you were bound for certain death.

James

Discussion Starters

1. Discuss together the Matthew 19 reading and both why you think Jesus said 'it is easier for a camel to go through the eye of a needle than for a rich man to enter the kingdom of God', and the disciples' response.

2. Is it right to equate poverty with spirituality? The Bible talks continually about God's blessing; does this include wealth and the prosperity gospel? Discuss these seeming tensions.

3. What are some of the ways in which people pursue wealth and seek to find status?

4. Discuss ways in which we can show favouritism and partiality to others and some of the motivations that cause us to do this.

Are you prejudiced?

WEEK THREE

5. What is the implication of the 'royal law'? Is it right that we should love ourselves? In the account of the Good Samaritan what did Jesus identify as the motivation? (See Luke 10:25–37, if possible in the AV)

6. Discuss the implications of the 11th (new) commandment that Jesus gave in John 13:34.

7. What is mercy and how does this differ from grace?

8. What specific steps is your church making to reach out to both the wealthy and the outcasts of society?

God's riches at Jesus' expense.

sorry thankyou please?

Personal Application

James Russell Lowell once said, 'We have gone on far too long on the principle "I am as good as you". This is the principle of selfishness that has made the world sick almost to death. We should act rather on the other principle, "You are as good as I", for this is the note of brotherhood and of humility which the Lord and His apostles first declared unto men.'

When we realise that we are all sinners in God's sight it doesn't matter whether people are rich or poor, commoner or prince, all need to know and experience the saving grace of Jesus. Be sure of this, there is no discrimination or favouritism at the foot of the cross.

Seeing Jesus in the Scriptures

Meekness is not weakness, and the image portrayed of 'gentle Jesus meek and mild' as being a timid, effeminate, timorous nature, could not be farther from the truth. The word meekness is a term of controlled strength, and was the term applied to tamed animals such as a lion, or a horse that had been broken in. These animals had just as much power and strength and ferocity, only now controlled and channelled. Jesus' meekness was not evidenced by letting people take advantage over Him, but in that it enabled him with all His kingly authority to willingly lay aside the power vested in Him, to assume the role of a humble servant. As the hymn goes, 'Hallelujah! What a Savior!'

WEEK FOUR
Faith on the move

Opening Icebreaker

Each member of the group should write down their name and an act of simple kindness they are capable of doing for another member. Put the entries in a basket and every member gets to pick one out and receive the kind act.

Bible Readings

- James 1:22–27; 2:14–25
- Matthew 5:13–16
- Luke 6:32–36; 10:25–37
- Philippians 2:1–4

Stressors: Self-interest and Personal Ambition

Stress and strain busters: Kindness and Goodness

Opening our Eyes

James now warms again to the subject of faith and action and further unpacks his thinking on *self-interest and personal ambition*. Who better to take note of, having lived with and observed Jesus the action man at close quarters, always doing good. Wherever He went something active happened, some tangible effect resulted for someone else, some life or circumstance was deeply changed and impacted.

Today the west is fast becoming nations of armchair observers, freely expressing our opinions and ideas in the comfort and protection of our own homes as events are brought right into our living rooms as they happen. Someone has said that the UK is becoming a nation of 'couch potatoes'. Observing, commentating, even being indignant, expressing outrage, or deep concern, but remaining uninvolved spectators, watching others, cheering them on, sympathising with them, but doing nothing about it ourselves. We are too busy, wrapped up in our own concerns.

Somebody else said, 'Evil triumphs when good men do nothing.' Is it possible that we have become 'pew potatoes', sitting in our comfortable modern churches listening to nice homilies, nodding or wagging our heads, yet remaining complacent, indifferent and uninvolved?

Faith brings salvation, but it is works, involvement in other people's lives, that demonstrates that salvation. Another person has said, 'I'd rather see a sermon than hear one any day.' True faith impacts conduct as well as character, and affects behaviour as well as belief.

'Faith and works' are like oars on a boat. If you continue to pull on just one you'll go round in circles, but if you pull on both oars equally at the same time you go forward and make

Faith on the move

for the shore where others await. Faith without works and, conversely, works without faith, are like a boat with one oar. They lack the dynamic life-changing thrust, and like a corpse after the spirit has departed is lifeless with no movement or action, so faith without works is dead and useless.

We all need to take steps to demonstrate our faith. The wonderful news of the gospel is that Christianity does work. How? By demonstrating that faith, in *acts of kindness and goodness*. That's right, helping others in practical and tangible ways.

When was the last time you laid aside your self-interest and personal ambition to provide hospitality, or gave someone elderly their lunch, or looked after children for a harassed mother, or took someone underprivileged out for a treat? When was the last time you gave until it hurt and stretched yourself to the point of sacrifice in order to bless someone else? I know these are challenging questions, but James pulls no punches, he was deadly serious about this business of active Christianity. Active obedience demonstrates genuine faith, so here are some steps to follow.

1. Make a commitment to do a specific act of kindness/good work at least once a week.
2. Decide on who the recipient/s should be.
3. Decide on the course of action/s to implement.
4. Evaluate what the cost/sacrifice will be and set it aside.
5. Plan your courses of action deliberately and carefully.
6. Determine not to look for credit or approval in the process.
7. Do it as unto the Lord, not looking for future reward or recognition.

James sums it up, 'Faith that doesn't show itself is no faith at all – it is dead and useless' (2:17, *The Living Bible*).

Discussion Starters

1. Think through and identify some of the good works Jesus did.

2. Discuss the concepts of earning our salvation and working out our salvation (Phil. 2:12).

3. Contrast the views of Paul in Romans 3:28 with James 2:18 and discuss whether these are contradictory or complementary.

4. Go back and look at the two Old Testament illustrations James gives: Abraham (Gen. 15:6; 22:1–14); and Rahab (Josh. 2:1–16; Heb. 11:31).

Faith on the move

WEEK | FOUR

5. What do you think of the possibility of some of us being described as 'pew potatoes'? What might be some of the characteristics to look for?

6. Look at James 2:19. Is James suggesting here that even demons have faith?

7. Break down into pairs, look at the seven steps and talk through together what you could do to implement them. You could then pray for each other.

8. We often say 'God bless you.' What about learning to say 'and I bless you too'? Think about it.

Personal Application

A book salesman excitedly approached a farmer. 'This book,' he said, 'will tell you absolutely everything you need to know about farming; when to sow, when to reap; all about the weather patterns and what to expect.' The farmer replied, 'But son, that's not my problem. I already know what's in the book, my problem is doing it!' In the Old Testament, the story is depicted in 2 Samuel 3:1–18 of Abner the prophet challenging the nation to accept David as their rightful king. His word to them was, *'Now do it.'* Need I say more!

Seeing Jesus in the Scriptures

When Peter preached to the Gentiles (Acts 10:34–48), he testified to Jesus by saying 'God anointed Jesus of Nazareth with the Holy Spirit and power, and how he went around doing good... We are witnesses of everything He did' Jesus had an urgency that compelled Him to work the works of God. He said, 'As long as it is day, we must do the work of him who sent me. Night is coming when no-one can work' (John 9:4). He also said, 'For the very work that the Father has given me to finish, and which I am doing, testifies that the Father has sent me' (John 5:36). Jesus expected those who come to faith in Him to continue carrying out His good works. He said, 'I tell you the truth, anyone who has faith in me will do what I have been doing. He will do even greater things than these, because I am going to the Father' (John 14:12).

WEEK FIVE

The taming of the tongue

Opening Icebreaker

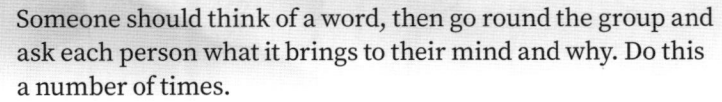

Someone should think of a word, then go round the group and ask each person what it brings to their mind and why. Do this a number of times.

Bible Readings

- James 3
- Psalm 34:8–14
- Proverbs 1:1–7; 2:6–12; 21:20–23
- 1 Peter 3:8–12

Stressors: Anger and Temper; Decisions and Choices

Stress and strain busters: Self-control and Christ-control; Wisdom and Discernment

Opening our Eyes

Having looked at the issue of actions, James returns to sharp words emanating from *anger and temper* and a lack of self-restraint and control. Christianity is a way of both acting and speaking and the best of actions can be undermined by negative words. Someone said, 'No one is converted until his tongue is converted.' How easy it is to insensitively offend others with our words. This raises two issues. How can we best avoid using destructive words, and if we fail, how can we handle the hurt we have caused?

James tells it like it is, the tongue is difficult to control. However, that doesn't let us off the hook. He says we control and tame wild animals, steer huge ships with small rudders, control horses with small bits, yet no human can tame the tongue. Ah, there you have it. It takes divine intervention to provide the necessary control of the tongue. Just like the bit and rudder, the tongue, although small, shapes and controls our lives. James says our words either bless or curse, delight or destroy, heal or hurt, comfort or cut.

It is not only learning to say the right thing at the right time, but also learning to control the desire to say what is unnecessary, unkind or inappropriate. Don't underestimate the awesome power of words. James says they can be like a fire out of control consuming and destroying everything in its path, and a poisonous viper full of venom, striking out suddenly, inflicting paralysis and death. How many hearts have been broken, reputations shattered and lives blighted, by an unruly tongue?

So how do we avoid using wrong words? With *self-control and Christ's control*. We set the guard over our lips, 'think before you speak', and as we are thinking, we ask God for His supply of wisdom. The choice is ours. We can yield the tongue to

Christ's control, trust Him for words of wisdom, then take control of our own words by asking the following questions:

- Is it a considered response?
- Is it hearsay or fact?
- Is it necessary?
- Am I overreacting?
- Do I have the right perspective?
- Am I exaggerating?
- Is it kind or hurtful?
- Will it bring peace or create turmoil?
- Will it build up or tear down?
- Will I say it graciously or harshly?

When it comes to decisions and choices, James highlights two kinds of wisdom: earthly and heavenly. Earthly wisdom is centred in human reasoning, motivated by self-interest, selfish ambition, pride and envy. The world says, assert yourself, be successful, you owe it to yourself to have this or to have that. The Old Testament puts it, 'They did everything that was right in their own eyes', and Frank Sinatra sang, 'I did it my way'. In God's eyes it is sheer foolishness. James says such wisdom is worldly, unspiritual, comes from the devil and leads to wrong decisions, confusion and strife.

He says 'Come on, wise up, there is another stream of *wisdom and discernment* available to us with characteristics so different.' True wisdom is God-given, carries eternal perspectives, is other-centred, with pure motives, a peaceable nature, a gentle approach and practical application. It is a wisdom that allows us to admit our failures and face them courageously. As we saw in an earlier chapter, we need to ask and avail ourselves of it, then courageously follow through with right choices and decisions. The blessing of wisdom is like a reservoir, it is always there to draw on.

Discussion Starters

1. What are some of the ways an untamed tongue expresses itself?

2. Get into twos or threes and share with each other things people have said that they found hurtful at the time and how they have resolved it.

3. James brings out the contradictory nature of the tongue in verse 9. Identify some of those contradictions.

4. When we do fail and say harsh words, how can we handle the hurt we have caused?

The taming of the tongue

WEEK FIVE

5. Look at the wisdom characteristic of being 'considerate'. The AV says 'easy to be intreated' (James 3:17). What does this imply?

6. What do you think 'full of mercy and good fruit' means, especially in relation to the use of the tongue (v17)?

7. Look at verse 17 and identify the eight characteristics of wisdom and the impact on our decisions and choices and words.

8. What are some of the different ways we can act as peacemakers?

Personal Application

James says 'we all stumble in many ways'. Whew, I'm not the only one then.

'If anyone is never at fault in what he says, he is a perfect man' (3:2). One way the tongue causes us to stumble is by exaggeration and embellishment. False rumours and malicious gossip that destroy people's lives and reputations develop this way. A note found in the hand of a suicide victim contained two words, 'They said' and was never completed. I wonder what caustic, corrosive words were said to drive that person to such drastic action?

The tongue has a natural tendency to exaggerate. Have you ever had a tooth removed that left a cavity, then felt the gap with your tongue? What a surprise when you looked in the mirror and found the space was so small. Don't allow your tongue to be the small spark setting a forest fire going with all its devastation. How easy it is to inflame a situation with an unguarded word.

Seeing Jesus in the Scriptures

Isaiah prophesied 'The Spirit of the Lord will rest on him – the Spirit of wisdom and of understanding' (Isa. 11:2). Luke records of the boy Jesus after His parents had discovered Him giving amazing answers to the Temple teachers, 'Jesus grew in wisdom and in stature' (Luke 2:52). The people of Nazareth were amazed and said, 'Where did this man get this wisdom?' (Matt. 13:54). Paul summed it up when he wrote to the Colossians 'Christ, in whom are hidden all the treasures of wisdom and knowledge' (Col. 2:3).

WEEK | SIX

WEEK SIX

To thine own self be true

Opening Icebreaker

Take the advertisements prepared and try to identify the product manufacturer and what they are trying to appeal to in us.

Bible Readings

- James 4; 3:14
- Exodus 20:17
- Psalm 143:8–10
- Luke 12:15
- 1 Peter 5:6–10

Stressors: Compromise and Self-deception; Temptation and Sin

Stress and strain busters: Honesty and Integrity; Vigilance and Resistance

Opening our Eyes

James commences this chapter continuing the theme of selfish ambition, when *compromise and self-deception* (building on 3:14–16) push us back down the track of achieving our own personal goals and desires. This, he says, leads to breakdown in personal relationships. The competitive dynamic that emerges sets us against each other. Quarrels and divisions follow as surely as night follows day.

He returns to the point again, that so often we don't take time to ask God for wisdom, and adds a further dimension that even when we do, we don't receive because our motivation is for personal benefit, self-indulgence, and is from the position of selfish ambition. He brings us straight to the core issue: covetousness, the plague of the modern age and central focus of the marketing media. Current advertising slogans appeal to this most basic human instinct that says, 'I have the right to have and to enjoy the same as others.'

What is covetousness? It is the unreasonable lust to acquire what we don't have, but long to; the desire to obtain what we cannot rightfully have to satisfy some inner need; a restless spirit of discontent leading to compromise and self-deception in justifying its pursuit.

There is something within us that wants to have and to hold. Advertisers target their products for comfort, status, recognition and selfish enjoyment, dressing them up in such a way as to motivate us to pursue and acquire them. They become 'must have' items we begin to covet for ourselves, and we deceive ourselves when we believe this. Isn't this what the modern craze for designer labels and state of the art, up-to-date gadgets and gismos is all about?

To thine own self be true

The weight of the mountain of personal debt in society comes from this self-deluded spirit of covetousness driving people to take out high cost loans, made so easily available, appealing to acquisitiveness and covetousness. Paul said 'the love of money is a root of all kinds of evil' (1 Tim. 6:10). It used to be that people tried to keep up with the Jones's, now they are not happy unless they've overtaken them! Yesterday's luxuries have become today's necessities. John put it this way, 'Don't love the world's ways. Don't love the world's goods. Love of the world squeezes out love for the Father. Practically everything that goes on in the world – wanting your own way, wanting everything for yourself, wanting to appear important – has nothing to do with the Father' (1 John 2:15–16, *The Message*).

Covetousness leads to relational breakdown through envy, jealousy and greed. Ultimately, James says, it leads to fights and quarrels. So don't let the devil gain an advantage in this way. The Personal Application section covers steps James outlines in dealing with *temptation and sin* and in defeating and overcoming the devil. Be *vigilant and resistant* against this insidious onslaught of the modern age. 'Don't be proud,' he says, 'humble yourself and God will give you grace to deal with it.' How? By resisting the devil's enticements.

The remainder of the chapter talks about moving on into the future, not in a presumptuous cavalier way, but in unencumbered *honesty and integrity*, humbly seeking God's direction and will. Life is short, he says, put aside brashness, self-importance and personal interest, always do what you know to be right and good, don't talk one way and live another, but demonstrate honesty and integrity in all your dealings; if you don't, you'll be continuing in sin.

Discussion Starters

1. Discuss how selfish ambition leads to competitive behaviour patterns, and identify some of these.

2. Explore the idea of God not answering our requests. Does it mean that if we ask with a pure motive God will answer our prayers?

3. What are some of the ways the media appeals to covetousness?

4. Discuss the definition of covetousness in the notes and look at verse 5 in relation to envy and the human condition. How does it relate to legitimate desire?

5. How can covetousness lead to compromise and self-deception?

To thine own self be true

6. What are some of yesterdays 'luxuries' that have become today's 'necessities'? Are they all really necessary?

---

7. Is it ever right to incur debt? Is debt always linked to covetousness?

---

8. Break down into pairs and consider the steps to overcoming the devil.

---

9. Talk about the dying habit of Christians to add in their conversation the phrase 'God willing'.

---

10. What is the practical outworking of honesty and integrity?

Personal Application

James gives practical insights, and in verses 7–10 outlines clear steps to follow in dealing with the devil and his temptations.

1. Submit yourself first to God.
2. Resist the devil and his devilish enticements.
3. Come near to God and feel the reality of His presence.
4. Wash your hands, by letting go of the things that have soiled them.
5. No longer allow your mind to be pulled in two directions.
6. Be sorry for allowing covetousness and if necessary weep over it.
7. Don't approach this light-heartedly, get serious.
8. Humble yourself in this matter, repent and God will raise you to new heights.
9. Refrain from judging or slandering others because of what they have.

Build these principles into your Christian life today.

Seeing Jesus in the Scriptures

'No test or temptation that comes your way is beyond the course of what others have had to face. All you need to remember is that God will never let you down; he'll never let you be pushed past your limit; he'll always be there to help you come through it' (1 Cor. 10:13, *The Message*). 'Now we know what we have – Jesus, this great High Priest with ready access to God – let's not let it slip through our fingers. We don't have a priest who is out of touch with our reality. He's been through weakness and testing, experienced it all – all but the sin. So let's walk right up to him and get what he is ready to give. Take the mercy, accept the help' (Heb. 4:15–16, *The Message*).

WEEK SEVEN

Patience is a virtue

Opening Icebreaker

Say together the Lord's Prayer.

Bible Readings

- James 5
- 1 Kings 18:41–45
- Job 42:8–16
- Psalm 37:1–7
- Romans 12:12
- Hebrews 2:1–3

Stressors: Trials and Adversity

Stress and strain busters: Patience, Perseverance and Prayer

Opening our Eyes

James starts his final chapter returning to the subject of status and wealth, highlighting the worthlessness of riches and warning the rich oppressors who had exploited and defrauded their workers, condemning them for their pursuit of luxury, vanity, self-indulgence and hoarding wealth. The lesson is that a selfish lifestyle inevitably leads to painful consequences. In the middle, he assures these early, oppressed believers that their *trial and adversity* has not escaped God's notice (v4) introducing the final theme, *patience and perseverance with prayer* in the face of adversity. Continual adversity can be like a dripping tap slowly driving us to despair. James says, 'Don't give up, be patient, persevere, remember Job and Elijah.'

We live in an impatient society, where demands are expected to be met immediately. Everything must be instant, from instant print, instant coffee, instant potatoes, to instant cash. It is the age of microwave mentality. So often we approach God with this level of expectation, wanting instant answers to prayers and instant changes to circumstances. God is viewed as some sort of cosmic vending machine, in goes the prayer out comes the answer and, like the 24-hour courier service, delivery must be by next morning.

The word patience comes from the two Latin words '*patior*', meaning 'I suffer' and '*sensio*' meaning 'with sense'. It means, 'facing suffering sensibly'. How do we make sense of life? Not by demanding immediate explanations and instant intervention and solutions, but by taking God's perspective, drawing on His supply of compassion and mercy that enables us to persevere. Patience is learned in the crucible of adversity. This process develops character, steadfastness and endurance. Paul puts it like this, 'we also rejoice in our sufferings, because we know that suffering produces perseverance; perseverance, character; and character, hope. And hope does not disappoint us, because God has poured his love into our hearts' (Rom. 5:3–5).

Steel is forged in the furnace, tempered on the anvil. The mighty oak grows best on windswept hills exposed to the elements, winds and rain. The blast of the storms forces its roots deeper and its branches grow stronger. The farmer cannot hurry his crop. He toils, breaking up the fallow ground, waiting diligently during the long, dark, harsh, winter months. There is a work of God going on in us in the bleakest times even though we may not recognise it. Like the farmer, be willing to work, wait and trust.

James says, If you are in trouble pray, if you are sick get the elders to anoint you and pray, confess your sins, pray for each other (vv13–18). Pray righteously – with pure motives, pray earnestly – with passion, pray persistently – constantly. Then believe the promises. The prayer of faith *will* make the sick person well, the Lord *will* raise them up, their sins *will* be forgiven, righteous prayer *is* powerful and effective, earnest prayer *brings* results and persistent prayers *open* the heavens.

Elijah called on God in the face of adversity, refused to give up, was patient, persistent and, through the power of prayer, overcame his impossible situation. You can too. Job, the model of patience, perseverance and overwhelming suffering, endured long, prayed for his friends and saw his circumstances change (Job 42:10).

James finishes his seminar on Christian Living recognising that, despite the keys he has given, some may succumb to the 'stresses and strains' and be overwhelmed by them. 'don't write them off,' he says. 'Go after them. Get them back and you will have rescued precious lives from destruction' (5:19–20, *The Message*).

Discussion Starters

1. Think about how you might pray if you were being exploited and defrauded by your rich oppressors. Would you do anything else?

2. What are some of the ways impatience reveals itself?

3. What do you think about the concept of patience meaning suffering sensibly?

4. Job is mentioned. Think of other biblical characters who suffered but showed patience. Who were some who were impatient?

5. What do you think the significance of anointing with oil is when praying for the sick?

Patience is a virtue

6. How do you feel about confessing your sins (AV – 'faults') to each other? Do you agree with the Catholic practice of the confessional?

7. Go back and look at the account of Elijah in 1 Kings 18:41–45 and discuss what praying earnestly – with passion – is.

8. Ask in the group if there are those they are aware of, who once ran well in the race of faith, but no longer seem to, then pray for them to be restored.

9. As we come to the end of this last study week on James, what has been the most significant thing in the study for you?

Personal Application

Be resolute, not double-minded or two-faced, mean yes when you say yes, and no when you mean no (v12). Some find it difficult to say no, because they've grown up in a culture of being people-pleasers. They harbour the underlying fear of rejection if they don't say yes, or feel guilty when turning people down. Others find it hard to say yes and commit themselves, having grown up in a culture of humiliation and ridicule. They harbour the underlying fear of failure and a sense of inadequacy so always say no. It's time for some to face those fears, bring them to the cross, surrender them to Christ and experience the release of saying no instead of yes just to please people – and for others, instead of automatically saying no, to be able to say yes and commit themselves.

Seeing Jesus in the Scriptures

Prayer is a learned habit, and was such a part of Jesus' life that the Gospels tell us that He prayed early in the morning (Mark 1:35), during the day (Luke 5:16), in the evening (Mark 6:46) and all night (Luke 6:12). The impact on the disciples was so great that they said to Jesus, 'Lord teach us to pray' and in response Jesus gave them the model prayer (Luke11:1–4). We often call this the Lord's Prayer, but in fact it is the disciples' prayer; He gave it to them. If you struggle with prayer, follow the disciples' lead and ask, 'Lord teach me to pray.' Begin to spend a few moments, morning, evening and during the day, in prayer.

Leader's Notes

Week One: Life stresses and strains

Opening Icebreaker
The idea of this exercise is to get the group identifying some of their daily pressures and giving them a non-threatening opportunity to talk about them.

Aim of the Session
To explore the first four daily life pressures that James identifies. The stress and strain busters are also identified. These are not dealt with here and will be the subject of the following weeks' studies.

Discussion Starter 1: Be sensitive here and don't put pressure on anyone in the group. You are not looking for problems to be shared but pressures such as workload, expectations, finances etc. Start by sharing one yourself to set the tone. This will lead you into discussing the pressures. The idea is to illustrate that we all live with pressures, but the issue is do we know how to handle them well? If a group member shares a deeper issue, gently steer them away from it by suggesting a more general daily pressure.

Discussion Starter 2: Looking at Paul's response to adversity, talk about learning to respond with grace rather than reacting to the pressure. Receiving grace changes our attitude. Rejoicing in our salvation doesn't minimise or negate adversity, it gives us strength and perspective in it. Point out that because we live in an instant society we expect God to deliver us now. Patience is the capacity to evidence calm assurance and composure in the midst of enduring pain and trying circumstances.

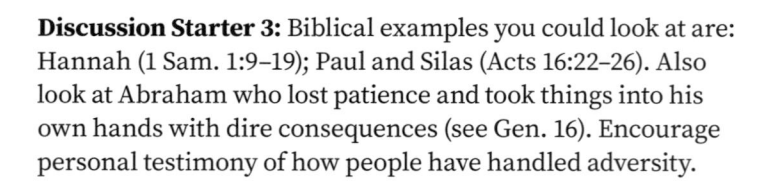

Discussion Starter 3: Biblical examples you could look at are: Hannah (1 Sam. 1:9–19); Paul and Silas (Acts 16:22–26). Also look at Abraham who lost patience and took things into his own hands with dire consequences (see Gen. 16). Encourage personal testimony of how people have handled adversity.

Discussion Starter 4: A good definition is, 'Wisdom is seeing life from God's point of view.' If we could see our trials and difficulties from God's point of view we would receive a whole new perspective and different meaning on life. See what the group comes up with; it should be interesting. God's Word is full of wisdom, and we can't ignore it by neglecting it, thinking that we can offer up an arrow prayer as a shortcut to the wisdom supply.

Discussion Starter 5: Draw out here that the human soul longs for a sense of acceptance and security and misguidedly looks for it in position and possession. When we come to Christ we are accepted in Him and secure in His love and purposes. Status and wealth no longer become pursuits, but blessings. Explore together how in their work environment people display their status and what kind of pressure that puts on them.

Discussion Starter 6: The key characteristic, a servant's heart, is illustrated in Philippians 2 and James 1:1. In John 13 Jesus took the position of a servant, picked up the towel and commenced washing His disciples' feet, reversing the role He traditionally had had with them. You might want to consider the possibility of having a foot-washing session with the group if you felt it appropriate.

Discussion Starter 7: To understand that temptation is not sin is the first step to dealing with temptation. Jesus was tempted in all points like us but did not succumb (Heb. 4:15; Matt. 4). Enticements are from without, but yielding to temptation

Leader's Notes

comes from within to satisfy the carnal nature's desires. It has been said, 'You can't stop the birds flying overhead, but you can stop them building nests in your hair.' The thing to bring out here is personal responsibility, that 'the devil made me do it' is not a valid excuse for yielding to temptation.

Week Two: Saints under pressure

Opening Icebreaker
The idea of this exercise is to illustrate the truth of verses 23–24. It is often easier to remember the features of another person's face than it is your own. That's why James says we must continue looking into the mirror of God's Word, so that we can get an accurate reflection of our own condition.

Aim of the Session
To continue to explore the daily life pressures that James identifies. As in the previous week the stress and strain busters are also identified and these will be the subject of the following weeks' studies.

To introduce this session, get the group to identify and recap on the four areas covered last week.

Discussion Starter 2: Move the discussion back to the wider group, getting them to identify what words they often use when they are expressing their anger. The thing to bring out here is that when we identify the words, we can take control over them. Also explore with them what other things accompany the words to give them added weight – things like a look, strength, expression, intonation, emphasis etc.

Discussion Starter 3: Bring out here the difference between self-control and repression. Repression is simply pushing the anger down to simmer and fester and accumulate with other unresolved anger, ready to burst out like a volcano later. The important thing to bring out here is that we need to take control of our anger. Self-control is taking responsibility not only by not giving vent to the anger, but by exploring what causes the anger, recognising it, acknowledging it, honestly exploring why you are feeling angry, confessing it to the Lord and repenting of it. If harsh words have been said, deal a blow to pride and ask the person concerned for forgiveness.

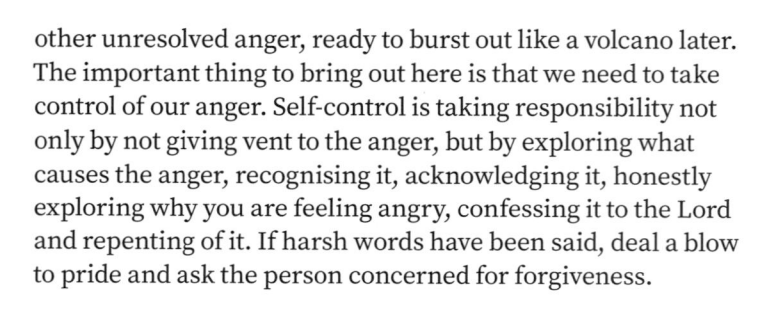

Discussion Starter 4: You're looking here to bring out the fact that the culture of our working environment is set by others, and that it is possible for us to accept their standards because that's the way it is. It is important to bring our own standards to bear in order to bring a stark contrast. Some of the issues might be: lateness, taking advantage of the employer, sharp practice, inaccurate product claims, irregular financial practices, cheating on personal allowances etc.

Discussion Starter 5: Biblical examples would be people like Joseph and Potiphar's wife, the three Hebrew boys put in the fiery furnace, Elijah standing up to Jezebel, Stephen before the Sanhedrin, Jesus before Pilate, Paul before Felix.

Discussion Starter 6: Get the group to count up the number of times the rich man referred to himself and remember that God considers our self-centred ambitions as 'sheer folly'.

Discussion Starter 7: Ambition is the strong desire for success. Together, look at Joshua 1:7–8 with 24:31 and draw out the fact that God wants His people to be successful, primarily in fulfilling His purposes. The key for Joshua's success and prospering (it is not written of many of Israel's leaders that the Israelites served the Lord all the days of their tenure) was that he spoke the Word, meditated on it and then acted according to it.

Leader's Notes

Discussion Starter 8: This might be by visiting some widows or doing acts of kindness like household chores, building maintenance, or organising a day out for children with no fathers etc.

Week Three: Are you prejudiced?

Opening Icebreaker
This should produce some lively discussion, and start to set the scene on favouritism and partiality.

Aim of the Session
To see how we can serve others in humility and meekness with no regard either to their standing in life or a personal agenda of our own.

Discussion Starter 1: Often we use Jesus' words as an excuse not to reach out to the wealthy, which James describes as discrimination or partiality. Jesus' words were in response to the rich young ruler, who was given the particular challenge to give away all his wealth to the poor. It was not a blanket edict or requirement for all wealthy followers of Jesus. James says we should not court the wealthy because of benefits they may bring, and also that we must not shun them because wealth may make it difficult for them to find faith. Explore the Ecclesiastes 3 reading.

Discussion Starter 2: The old adage repeated when a minister was invited to a new parish was 'Lord you keep him humble, we'll keep him poor.' Spirituality does not mean poverty but dependence on God, knowing 'my God will meet all your needs according to his glorious riches in Christ Jesus' (Phil. 4:19). Paul also said, 'I know what it is to be in need, and I know what it is to have plenty' (Phil. 4:12). On the other hand prosperity doesn't signify God's blessing; there are many reasons why people are prosperous. God's blessing isn't measured on the scale of material assets.

Discussion Starter 3: People do strange things for recognition and fortune, like appearing on *Big Brother*, cheating on *Who Wants To Be A Millionaire*, or being humiliated on *The Weakest Link*. Others take shortcuts like Lotto, or are career-driven to acquire cars, houses, boats, buy titles, commendations etc.

Discussion Starter 4: Favouritism is shown by how we treat people, our attitudes on social standing, education, race, religion, skin colour, politics, disability, theological persuasion and prejudices from our upbringing, often motivated by feelings of superiority, feeling threatened, ignorance, personal gain or our own insecurities.

Discussion Starter 5: This verse is sometimes used as the basis of the need for self-acceptance and self-love – that if we love ourselves first, we will be able to love our neighbour. This is not what Jesus is implying (Matt. 19:18), as in fact he told the young man concerned to give everything he had to the poor and needy. They were the focus, not self. The important thing is, not that we love ourselves but that we accept ourselves in Christ, seeing ourselves as He does. We do not wait until we have sorted out our own issues of low self-image and feelings of inadequacy before loving others. We love with the love of Christ that supersedes our own deficiencies, not in our own strength. Christ's love is always other-centred as illustrated in Luke 10:30–37.

Discussion Starter 6: Jesus took the issue even further than the 'royal law', setting an even higher standard. Look at this, considering what lengths and depths Jesus went to in demonstrating that love.

Discussion Starter 7: Grace is God's free unmerited favour

Leader's Notes

that makes His supernatural provision, sustaining power and enabling strength available to us in all of life's circumstances. Mercy relates to judgment. Willingness is when somebody has committed an offence and is completely in the wrong, to show clemency, wipe the slate clean with forgiveness and completely restore. Jesus said, 'Blessed are the merciful, for they will be shown mercy' (Matt. 5:7).

Discussion Starter 8: This is an opportunity as a group to think up some ways of outreach to these sectors of the community.

Week Four: Faith on the move

Opening Icebreaker
The idea here is to get members of the group to do something for each other. It may be possible to do it right away, or maybe later. Things like cleaning shoes, ironing, giving a lift, babysitting…

Aim of the Session
To consider how we can carry out acts of kindness and goodness to bless others as a demonstration of our faith.

Discussion Starter 1: The group should identify some of the healings like the blind man, Jairus' daughter and the leper; some of the miracles, eg the water into wine, the multiplication of the loaves and fishes, stilling the storm etc, some personal encounters, such as the woman at the well, the Emmaus road disciples, visiting Mary, Martha and Lazarus at Bethany.

Discussion Starter 2: The gospel of good works is one many nominal Christians ascribe to. They immerse themselves in charitable works and good causes believing they are good people and that it will be sufficient for their salvation. Paul is saying that once we have allowed Christ to work in us His redeeming grace, then we need to work that salvation out in practice.

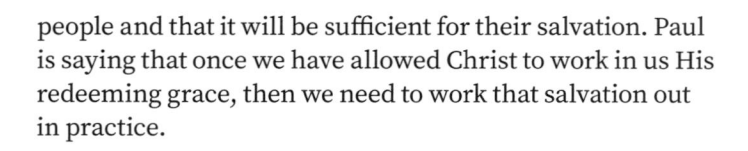

Discussion Starter 3: Point out it would be difficult for James to be contradicting Paul as at the time James wrote, Paul had yet to finish the first line of his many epistles. James and Paul are not at odds here. Paul speaks out against those seeking to earn their salvation through the process of good works. James speaks out against those who intellectually embrace the faith for their own reasons giving only mental assent and agreement to Christian teaching: a head knowledge lacking a heart conviction. He emphasises the difference between real faith and mere words, and is in no way implying salvation can be earned through good works.

Discussion Starter 4: James says that righteousness was counted to Abraham as a result of what he did and Paul in Romans 4:1–5 says it was for what he believed, thus giving two sides of the same coin. Rahab (Heb. 11:31) likewise demonstrates a clear faith, by the very actions she carried out bringing about both her own salvation and also her family's. God accepted Abraham and Rahab not only because they said they believed Him, but because they proved it by the actions they took.

Discussion Starter 5: Couch potato is now a phrase in common usage to describe a particular type of person. This is someone who is usually lethargic, makes themselves very comfortable in front of the TV, enjoys being entertained, feeds themselves to excess, is often over-weight, spends hours doing nothing practical, and escapes reality by indulging in a fantasy world. Together consider these characteristics from a church/spiritual angle.

Leader's Notes

Discussion Starter 6: James says it is possible to believe in the existence of God, or about God as a person and that even the demons recognise and acknowledge His presence. It makes them shudder or, as the King James Version says, 'tremble' and so it should. But that is insufficient, as saving faith has more to it than acknowledgement of existence. True and genuine faith involves a commitment of your whole self to God and has the consequence of being viewable by the ensuing change in character and the expression of good deeds.

Discussion Starter 8: Encourage the group to talk through some of the things you might be able to do practically to bless others.

Week Five: The taming of the tongue

Opening Icebreaker
This exercise is known as free association and illustrates that words conjure up different things for different people for different reasons, some positive and some negative.

Aim of the Session
To look at controlling the tongue and accessing divine wisdom in all our choices and decisions. Draw attention to the stressors and the stress and strain busters you are exploring this week.

Discussion Starter 1: You are looking for things like gossiping, duplicity, deceit, putting others down, slander, backbiting, cursing, flattery, exaggerating, bragging, complaining, negativity etc.

Discussion Starter 2: Some might find this difficult. Be sensitive and don't pressurise anyone who feels unable to share. After the small group sharing ask if there is anyone who might like to reflect to the larger group. After someone has done this ask if others in the group identify with them. You could start this off by sharing something yourself first.

Discussion Starter 3: This can happen when we say one thing to someone's face and another behind his or her back, or when we say something critical when someone has done something well because we are feeling threatened, or by affirming one thing in church but not in the workplace.

Discussion Starter 4: Responses you are looking for are:
- Accept personal responsibility for our words.
- Be quick to apologise.
- Be willing to ask for forgiveness.
- Take immediate steps to correct any misinformation.
- Rebuild any damage caused to a reputation.
- Start to speak positive and affirmative words of those concerned.
- Resist justifying ourselves, excusing ourselves or blaming others.
- Recognise that as well as self-control we need Christ-control.

Discussion Starter 5: Bring out the element of gentleness as not meaning weakness. It is not the allowing of an inferiority complex to show itself in a self-deprecating 'use me as a doormat' way. It is showing and giving the respect and sensitivity a person deserves when being approached and spoken to. 'Easy to be intreated' means being approachable, showing a warm, accepting, non-judgmental attitude of humility, demonstrating a willingness to listen and understand, not being distant, superior, detached or threatening. This is a strength not a weakness.

Leader's Notes

Discussion Starter 6: Words of mercy are shown when a person deserves condemnation or judgment over a mistake, failure or sin they have committed. Confronting people with gentleness does not mean we are not firm in pointing out their fault or responsibility in the matter, but we demonstrate grace and mercy by words of tolerance, forgiveness, affirmation. The words of good fruit are following that up with positive encouragement and support, committing ourselves to appropriate practical help.

Discussion Starter 7: Together think through the practical outworking of these characteristics in their decision-making and choices. For example, *pure*, the choice of what we read, the choice not to engage in smutty conversation; *submissive*, the decision to obey our superiors at work when we don't particularly like them, the choice not to answer back when we know we are right.

Discussion Starter 8: Usually disharmony is clouded in a war of words that obscures the actual issues. A peacemaker is impartial, doesn't take sides and brings perspective through words of conciliation. A peacemaker must be a peace minister which means that they must be at peace with themselves. You can't minister peace to others if you have not received that peace for yourself. The outcome of peacemaking, James says, is a 'harvest of righteousness'. Righteousness here implies right relationships, restored relationships, first with God, right standing with Him, then making things right with each other. A peacemaker serves in the role of mediator to bring about reconciliation. Jesus said, 'Blessed are the peacemakers' (Matt. 5:9).

Week Six: To thine own self be true

Opening Icebreaker
You will need to remove about 6–10 pages from magazines with some well-known branded products that appeal, such as cars, holidays, clothes, cosmetics, drinks, food, sport, health. Cut out the brand names from the advertisements so they are not readily identifiable. Number each one, pass them round the group asking them to note on a piece of paper the brand and what the advertisers are appealing to, such as image, status, pleasure, comfort, acceptance, machismo, sexiness etc. Take feedback into the main group.

Aim of the Session
To see how envy leads us to compromise and self-deceit when we give in to its enticements rather than resisting its allurements, and that vigilance, resistance, honesty and integrity of heart will keep us free from its clutches.

Remind the group of the stressors and stress and strain busters we are looking at this week.

Discussion Starter 1: Selfish ambition usually has little regard for others and its end goal is usually personal gain often at the expense of someone else. The competitive spirit emerges seeking to outdo everyone else in an effort to get to the top or be the best. Behaviour patterns can emerge such as bragging, putting others down, inflating achievements, cutting corners, outdoing others, becoming an overachiever, superiority complex, over-inflated ego, being a driven person. The Christian approach is to give of our best, learn from our mistakes and allow God to promote us according to His purposes. We do not always have to be striving and competing, living under the pressure it brings.

Leader's Notes

Discussion Starter 2: The point to bring out here is that selfish praying will be ignored by the almighty, like the boy who prayed 'Lord give me a wife but make sure it's Mary.' It does not mean that if we don't get an apparent answer to our prayers that they have been self-centred. Timing and trust are involved in prayer, and if our motives are pure, God will always answer, although not always in the way we might expect. Remember, Father knows best.

Discussion Starter 3: By making us dissatisfied with our current lot, and by presenting things that appeal to our ego, elevate us in the eyes of others and enhance our lifestyles. It focuses on things such as fashion, possessions, finances, looks, class, education, culture etc.

Discussion Starter 4: Get the group to look at the three components included in paragraph three. Discontent, the unreasonable lust to acquire, and the desire to obtain what we cannot rightfully have. A biblical illustration would be Deuteronomy 5:21. Legitimate desire is found in the words of Jesus 'But seek first his kingdom and his righteousness, and all these things will be given to you as well' (Matt. 6:33).

Discussion Starter 5: When we are so blinded to covetousness, we go to great lengths to get what we want, even compromising our principles and convictions for the sake of expediency in the process. We deceive ourselves by believing that the end justifies the means to obtain it.

Discussion Starter 6: Things like a washing machine, dishwasher, telephone, television, electric shaver, hairdryer etc.

Discussion Starter 7: Discuss together the debt culture in the light of Romans 13:8.

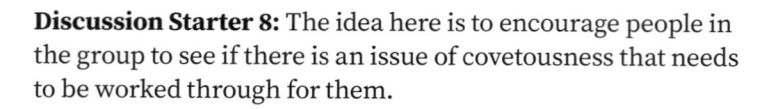

Discussion Starter 8: The idea here is to encourage people in the group to see if there is an issue of covetousness that needs to be worked through for them.

Discussion Starter 9: Those in the group who grew up with this as part of their early Christian teaching could talk about it.

Discussion Starter 10: It is using the plumb line of Scripture as a constant measure.

Week Seven: Patience is a virtue

Opening Icebreaker
Invite group members to add their own prayers after the Lord's Prayer.

Aim of the Session
The aim of this final study is to draw together the insights of James with the undergirding values of patience and prayer.

Discussion Starter 1: The responses might be, to pray for their 'oppressors' for a change of heart, for salvation, to pray for themselves for grace, patience, wisdom and right attitudes and to respond with obedience and faithfulness (Col. 3:22-25), respect (1 Tim. 6:1; 1 Pet. 2:18), trying to please their masters (Titus 2:9) by giving of their best (Eccl. 9:10).

Discussion Starter 2: Get some general responses such as, on the roads, waiting in queue's, the hurry hurry syndrome, the must have now generation etc. Then go round the group and ask what makes them impatient. You may get responses like: the checkout at the food shop, the person in front of you at the bank when you are paying in your weekly takings, your own lateness, waiting for an important letter,

Leader's Notes

singing choruses umpteen times when you want to hear 'the Word' etc.

Discussion Starter 3: Draw out the fact that suffering doesn't make sense and also that it is hard to make sense of our own suffering unless it is self-inflicted. Patience is not trying to make sense of suffering, but learning to approach the suffering with acceptance and awareness and a realistic reasonable assessment of the circumstances. It is the capacity to calmly endure emotional, physical and spiritual discomfort, and the willingness to wait while it runs its course. This does not mean we resign ourselves to it in a fatalistic way, but that we learn to draw on God's resources to endure it with grace and persevere with courage.

Discussion Starter 4: There are many like Noah, Joseph, Daniel, Moses, Jeremiah, David. Impatient ones include Abraham, Jonah, Naaman, the Israelites.

Discussion Starter 5: Some commentators believe that in biblical times oil was used for its medicinal purpose in the healing process and that it was often applied externally for this purpose. Jesus talked about oil and wine being poured into the wounds of the Samaritan (Luke 10:34). Others believe that it was a symbolic gesture signifying the combination of both prayer and medicine together in bringing healing. Another view is that oil is a symbol of the Holy Spirit in Scripture and the oil here denotes the intervention of the work of the Spirit in the healing process. The oil was blessed or consecrated, but the important thing is that it is the prayer of faith that brings the healing rather than the oil.

Discussion Starter 6: Be sensitive with this as some will feel threatened by it. It is daunting for many because of the fear of being exposed and condemned by others for their lapses and failures. They are afraid that others will be shocked and point the finger of accusation at them. Could this be why some of our church relationships are so shallow and brittle, because we are not willing to be vulnerable with each other? James says that far from pointing the finger, we need to pray for each other to be healed.

Discussion Starter 7: When we are passionate about something, we feel deeply and strongly about it. There is both an enthusiasm and an emotional involvement that create intense desire. We become gripped with the cause, expressing it openly and fervently. Often our praying can be detached and perfunctory. Elijah put his head between his knees, shutting everything around him out, putting all of his focus and energies into his prayer.

Discussion Starter 8: Spend time praying together for any who are mentioned.

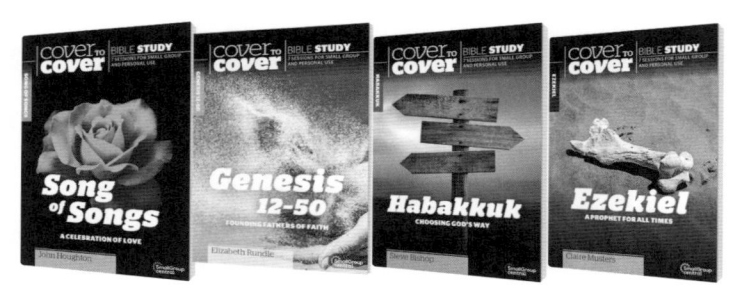

The *Cover to Cover* Bible Study Series

1 Corinthians
Growing a Spirit-filled church
ISBN: 978-1-85345-374-8

2 Corinthians
Restoring harmony
ISBN: 978-1-85345-551-3

1,2,3 John
Walking in the truth
ISBN: 978-1-78259-763-6

1 Peter
Good reasons for hope
ISBN: 978-1-78259-088-0

2 Peter
Living in the light of God's promises
ISBN: 978-1-78259-403-1

23rd Psalm
The Lord is my shepherd
ISBN: 978-1-85345-449-3

1 Timothy
Healthy churches – effective Christians
ISBN: 978-1-85345-291-8

2 Timothy and Titus
Vital Christianity
ISBN: 978-1-85345-338-0

Abraham
Adventures of faith
ISBN: 978-1-78259-089-7

Acts 1–12
Church on the move
ISBN: 978-1-85345-574-2

Acts 13–28
To the ends of the earth
ISBN: 978-1-85345-592-6

Barnabas
Son of encouragement
ISBN: 978-1-85345-911-5

Bible Genres
Hearing what the Bible really says
ISBN: 978-1-85345-987-0

Daniel
Living boldly for God
ISBN: 978-1-85345-986-3

David
A man after God's own heart
ISBN: 978-1-78259-444-4

Ecclesiastes
Hard questions and spiritual answers
ISBN: 978-1-85345-371-7

Elijah
A man and his God
ISBN: 978-1-85345-575-9

Elisha
A lesson in faithfulness
ISBN: 978-1-78259-494-9

Ephesians
Claiming your inheritance
ISBN: 978-1-85345-229-1

Esther
For such a time as this
ISBN: 978-1-85345-511-7

Ezekiel
A prophet for all times
ISBN: 978-1-78259-836-7

Fruit of the Spirit
Growing more like Jesus
ISBN: 978-1-85345-375-5

Galatians
Freedom in Christ
ISBN: 978-1-85345-648-0

Genesis 1–11
Foundations of reality
ISBN: 978-1-85345-404-2

Genesis 12–50
Founding fathers of faith
ISBN: 978-1-78259-960-9

God's Rescue Plan
Finding God's fingerprints on human history
ISBN: 978-1-85345-294-9

Great Prayers of the Bible
Applying them to our lives today
ISBN: 978-1-85345-253-6

Habakkuk
Choosing God's way
ISBN: 978-1-78259-843-5

Haggai
Motivating God's people
ISBN: 978-1-78259-686-8

Hebrews
Jesus – simply the best
ISBN: 978-1-85345-337-3

Isaiah 1–39
Prophet to the nations
ISBN: 978-1-85345-510-0

Isaiah 40–66
Prophet of restoration
ISBN: 978-1-85345-550-6

Jacob
Taking hold of God's blessing
ISBN: 978-1-78259-685-1

James
Faith in action
ISBN: 978-1-85345-293-2

Jeremiah
The passionate prophet
ISBN: 978-1-85345-372-4

John's Gospel
Exploring the seven miraculous signs
ISBN: 978-1-85345-295-6

Jonah
Rescued from the depths
ISBN: 978-1-78259-762-9

Joseph
The power of forgiveness and reconciliation
ISBN: 978-1-85345-252-9

Joshua 1-10
Hand in hand with God
ISBN: 978-1-85345-542-7

Judges 1-8
The spiral of faith
ISBN: 978-1-85345-681-7

Judges 9-21
Learning to live God's way
ISBN: 978-1-85345-910-8

Luke
A prescription for living
ISBN: 978-1-78259-270-9

Mark
Life as it is meant to be lived
ISBN: 978-1-85345-233-8

Mary
The mother of Jesus
ISBN: 978-1-78259-402-4

Moses
Face to face with God
ISBN: 978-1-85345-336-6

Names of God
Exploring the depths of God's character
ISBN: 978-1-85345-680-0

Nehemiah
Principles for life
ISBN: 978-1-85345-335-9

Parables
Communicating God on earth
ISBN: 978-1-85345-340-3

Philemon
From slavery to freedom
ISBN: 978-1-85345-453-0

Philippians
Living for the sake of the gospel
ISBN: 978-1-85345-421-9

Prayers of Jesus
Hearing His heartbeat
ISBN: 978-1-85345-647-3

Proverbs
Living a life of wisdom
ISBN: 978-1-85345-373-1

Revelation 1-3
Christ's call to the Church
ISBN: 978-1-85345-461-5

Revelation 4-22
The Lamb wins! Christ's final victory
ISBN: 978-1-85345-411-0

Rivers of Justice
Responding to God's call to righteousness today
ISBN: 978-1-85345-339-7

Ruth
Loving kindness in action
ISBN: 978-1-85345-231-4

The Armour of God
Living in His strength
ISBN: 978-1-78259-583-0

The Beatitudes
Immersed in the grace of Christ
ISBN: 978-1-78259-495-6

The Creed
Belief in action
ISBN: 978-1-78259-202-0

The Divine Blueprint
God's extraordinary power in ordinary lives
ISBN: 978-1-85345-292-5

The Holy Spirit
Understanding and experiencing Him
ISBN: 978-1-85345-254-3

The Image of God
His attributes and character
ISBN: 978-1-85345-228-4

The Kingdom
Studies from Matthew's Gospel
ISBN: 978-1-85345-251-2

The Letter to the Colossians
In Christ alone
ISBN: 978-1-855345-405-9

The Letter to the Romans
Good news for everyone
ISBN: 978-1-85345-250-5

The Lord's Prayer
Praying Jesus' way
ISBN: 978-1-85345-460-8

The Prodigal Son
Amazing grace
ISBN: 978-1-85345-412-7

The Second Coming
Living in the light of Jesus' return
ISBN: 978-1-85345-422-6

The Sermon on the Mount
Life within the new covenant
ISBN: 978-1-85345-370-0

Thessalonians
Building Church in changing times
ISBN: 978-1-78259-443-7

The Ten Commandments
Living God's Way
ISBN: 978-1-85345-593-3

The Uniqueness of our Faith
What makes Christianity distinctive?
ISBN: 978-1-85345-232-1

For current prices or to order, visit **cwr.org.uk/shop**
Available online or from Christian bookshops.

Be inspired by God.
Every day.

Confidently face life's challenges by equipping yourself daily with God's Word. There is something for everyone...

Every Day with Jesus
Selwyn Hughes' renowned writing is updated by Mick Brooks into these trusted and popular notes.

Life Every Day
Jeff Lucas helps apply the Bible to life through his trademark humour and insight.

Inspiring Women Every Day
Encouragement, uplifting scriptures and insightful daily thoughts for women.

The Manual
A straight-talking guide to help men walk with God. Written by Carl Beech.

To find out more about all our daily Bible reading notes, or to take out a subscription, visit **cwr.org.uk/biblenotes** or call 01252 784700.
Also available in Christian bookshops.

Printed format   Large print format   Email format   Ebook format

SmallGroup central

All of our small group ideas and resources in one place

Online:

smallgroupcentral.org.uk
is filled with free video teaching, tools, articles and a whole host of ideas.

On the road:

A range of seminars themed for small groups can be brought to your local community. Contact us at **hello@smallgroupcentral.org.uk**

In print:

Books, study guides and DVDs covering an extensive list of themes, Bible books and life issues.

Find out more at:
smallgroupcentral.org.uk

TRANSFORMED LIVING

TRANSFORMED LIFE

cover to cover

Every Day with Jesus extra

40 days with JESUS

Liz Babbs STUDY GUIDE

Life JOURNEYS

vital:

ToolBox

Courses and events

Waverley Abbey College

Publishing and media

Conference facilities

Transforming lives

CWR's vision is to enable people to experience personal transformation through applying God's Word to their lives and relationships.

Our Bible-based training and resources help people around the world to:
- Grow in their walk with God
- Understand and apply Scripture to their lives
- Resource themselves and their church
- Develop pastoral care and counselling skills
- Train for leadership
- Strengthen relationships, marriage and family life

and much more.

Our insightful writers provide daily Bible reading notes and other resources for all ages, and our experienced course designers and presenters have gained an international reputation for excellence and effectiveness.

CWR's Training and Conference Centre in Surrey, England, provides excellent facilities in an idyllic setting – ideal for both learning and spiritual refreshment.

CWR Applying God's Word to everyday life and relationships

CWR, Waverley Abbey House,
Waverley Lane, Farnham,
Surrey GU9 8EP, UK

Telephone: **+44 (0)1252 784700**
Email: info@cwr.org.uk
Website: www.cwr.org.uk

Registered Charity No. 294387
Company Registration No. 1990308